Jesus and Nonviolence

FACETS

Selected Titles in the Facets Series

Jesus and Nonviolence

A Third Way

Walter Wink

Fortress Press
Minneapolis

JESUS AND NONVIOLENCE
A Third Way

Portions of this book are developed from the author's *Violence and Nonviolence in South Africa: Jesus' Third Way* (Philadelphia: New Society Publishers, 1987), published in cooperation with the Fellowhip of Reconciliation.

Scripture quotations from the New Revised Standard Version of the Bible are copyright © 1989 by the Division of Christian Education of the National Council of the Churches of Christ in the United States of America and are used by permission.

Scripture quotations from the Revised Standard Version of the Bible, copyright © 1946, 1952, 1971 by the Division of Christian Education of the National Council of the Churches of Christ in the USA are used by permission.

Scripture quotations from The New English Bible, copyright © 1961, 1970 by the Delegates of the Oxford University Press and the Syndics of the Cambridge University Press are reprinted by permission.

Cover image: Abstract image of distorted light. A20FB8/Alamy. Used by permission.
Cover and book design: Joseph P. Bonyata
Author photo: Tricia Bergland

ISBN: 978-0-8006-3609-8

The paper used in this publication meets the minimum requirements of American National Standard for Information Sciences—Permanence of Paper for Printed Library Materials, ANSI Z329.48-1984.

Manufactured in the U.S.A.

Contents

Chapter 1

There have been some remarkable success stories of nonviolent struggle around the world recently. In the Philippines, a nonviolent revolution led by Corazon Aquino with crucial support from the churches swept the dictator Ferdinand Marcos from office with a loss of only 121 lives. Central to the effectiveness of that struggle was a background of training in nonviolent direct action provided by the International Fellowship of Reconciliation.

In Poland, Solidarity irreversibly mobilized popular sentiment against the puppet Communist regime. An entire clandestine culture, literature, and spirituality came to birth there outside the authority of official society. This undercuts the oft-repeated claim that what Mohandas Gandhi did in India or Martin Luther King Jr. did in the American South would never work under a brutal, Soviet-sponsored government.

Nonviolent general strikes have overthrown at least seven Latin American dictators: Carlos Ibáñez del Campo of Chile (1931), Gerardo Machado y Morales of Cuba (1933), Jorge Ubico of Guatemala (1944), Elie Lescot of Haiti (1946), Arnulfo Arias of Panama (1951), Paul Magliore of Haiti (1956), and Gustavo Rojas Pinilla of Colombia (1957).[1] In 1989-90 alone, fourteen nations underwent nonviolent revolutions, all of them successful except China, and all of them nonviolent except Romania. These revolutions involved 1.7 billion people. If we total all the nonviolent movements of the twentieth century, the figure comes to 3.4 billion people, and again, most were successful. And yet there are people who still insist that nonviolence doesn't work! Gene Sharp has itemized 198 different types of nonviolent actions that are a part of the historical record, yet our history books

we focus more on the
wayward violent acts than
taking nonviolent actions
to get a better result

seldom mention any of them, so preoccupied are they with power politics and wars.[2]

There are good reasons for reluctance to champion nonviolence. The term itself is negative. It sounds like a not-doing, the putting of all one's energy into avoiding something bad rather than throwing one's total being into doing something good. But the term itself is hardly the cause of objection. "Nonviolence" is identified by many as the injunction to be submissive before the authorities.[3] Romans 13:1-7 has been interpreted as an absolute command to obey the government *whatever it does.* "Turn the other cheek" became a divine ultimatum to slaves and servants to accept flogging and blows obsequiously. "Love of enemies" was twisted to render the oppressed compliant from the very heart, forgiving every injustice with no thought of changing the system. Nonviolence meant, in the context of this perverse inversion of the gospel, passivity. And the fact that "pacifism" and "passivism" sound so alike only made confusion worse.[4]

Nonviolence was seen as people submitting to those higher up and accepting what was happening around them.

Most Christians desire nonviolence, yes; but they are not talking about a nonviolent struggle for justice. They mean simply the absence of conflict. They would like the system to change without having to be involved in changing it. What they mean by nonviolence is as far from Jesus' third way as a lazy nap in the sun is from a confrontation in which protesters are being clubbed to the ground.

When a church that has not lived out a costly identification with the oppressed offers to mediate between hostile parties, it merely adds to the total impression that it wants to stay above the conflict and not take sides. The church says to the lion and the lamb, "Here, let me negotiate a truce," to which the lion replies, "Fine, after I finish my lunch."

"Reconciliation" also has been misused. Reconciliation is necessary, and it must be engaged in at all stages of the struggle. The human quality of the opponent must be continually affirmed. Some kind of trust that can serve as the basis of the new society to come must be established even in the midst of conflict. But when church leaders preach reconciliation without having unequivocally committed themselves to struggle on the side of the oppressed for justice, they are caught straddling a (pseudo-neutrality) made of nothing but thin air. Neutrality in a situation of oppression always supports the status quo. Reduction of conflict by means of a phony "peace" is not a Christian goal. Justice is the goal, and that may require an *acceleration* of conflict as a necessary stage in forcing those in power to bring about genuine change.

[margin handwriting: false]

[margin handwriting: may need conflict to reach the Goal]

Likewise, blanket denunciations of violence by the churches place the counterviolence of the oppressed on the same level as the violence of the system that has driven the oppressed to such desperation. Are stones thrown by youth really commensurate with buckshot and real bullets fired by police?

Finally, some pacifists have been rightly criticized for being more concerned with their own righteousness than with the sufferings of the afflicted. As Dietrich Bonhoeffer argued:

To maintain one's innocence in a setting such as that of the Third Reich, even to the point of *not* plotting Hitler's death, would be irresponsible action. To refuse to engage oneself in the demands of *necessita,* would be the selfish act of one who cared for his own innocence, who cared for his own guiltlessness, more than he cared for his guilty brothers.[5]

The issue is not, "What must I do in order to secure my salvation?" but rather, "What does God require of me in response to the needs of others?" It is not, "How can I be virtuous?" But "How can I participate in the struggle of the oppressed for a more just world?" Otherwise our nonviolence is premised on self-justifying attempts to establish our own purity in the eyes of God, others, and ourselves, and that is nothing less than a satanic temptation to die with clean hands and a dirty heart.[6]

For Discussion

1. What objections do you have to nonviolence?

2. Do you think you could be nonviolent, if not consistently, then during a specific demonstration or vigil?
3. What reasons can you find for choosing to be nonviolent?

← Don't just focus on yourself to save your face in the eyes of God. It is better to get your hands dirty and have your heart be free of guilt when you are helping the oppressed rather than due not sacrificing yourself for the cause of many.

Chapter 2

Many of those who have committed their lives to ending injustice simply dismiss Jesus' teachings <u>about non-violence out of hand as impractical idealism.</u> And with good reason. "Turn the other cheek" suggests the passive, Christian doormat quality that has made so many Christians cowardly and complicit in the face of injustice. "Resist not evil" seems to break the back of all opposition to evil and to counsel submission. "Going the second mile" has become a platitude meaning nothing more than "extend yourself," and rather than fostering structural change, encourages collaboration with the oppressor.

Jesus obviously never behaved in any of these ways. Whatever the source of the

nonviolence can be seen as more of giving oneself rather than taking what is owed.

misunderstanding, it is clearly in neither Jesus nor his teaching, which, when given a fair hearing in its original social context, is arguably one of the most revolutionary political statements ever uttered:

> You have heard that it was said, "An eye for an eye and a tooth for a tooth." But I say to you, Do not resist an evildoer. But if anyone strikes you on the right cheek, turn the other also; and if anyone wants to sue you and take your coat, give your cloak as well; and if anyone forces you to go one mile, go also the second mile (Matt. 5:38-41 NRSV).

When the court translators working in the hire of King James chose to translate *antistēnai* as "*Resist* not evil," they were doing something more than rendering Greek into English. They were translating nonviolent resistance into docility. Jesus did *not* tell his oppressed hearers not to resist evil. That would have been absurd. His entire ministry is utterly at odds with such a preposterous idea. The Greek word is made up of two parts: *anti,* a word still used in English for "against," and *histēmi,* a verb that in its noun form (*stasis*) means violent rebellion, armed revolt, sharp dissention. In the Greek Old Testament, *antistēnai* is used primarily for military encounters—44 out of 71 times. It refers specifically to the moment two armies collide, steel on steel, until one side breaks and flees. In the New Testament it describes Barabbas, a rebel "who had committed murder in the *insurrection*" (Mark 15:7; Luke 23:19, 25), and the townspeople in Ephesus, who "are in danger of being charged with *rioting*" (Acts 19:40). The term generally refers to a potentially lethal disturbance or armed revolution.[7]

A proper translation of Jesus' teaching would then be, "Don't strike back at evil (or, one who has done you evil) in kind." "Do not retaliate against violence with violence." The Scholars Version is brilliant: "Don't react violently against the one who is evil." Jesus was no less committed to opposing evil than the anti-Roman resistance fighters. The only

[handwritten margin note: Jesus' teachings were misunderstood. They twisted his words to suit their needs.]

difference was over the means to be used: *how* one should fight evil.

There are three general responses to evil: (1) passivity, (2) violent opposition, and 3) the third way of militant nonviolence articulated by Jesus. Human evolution has conditioned us for only the first two of these responses: flight or fight. "Fight" had been the cry of Galileans who had abortively rebelled against Rome only two decades before Jesus spoke. Jesus and many of his hearers would have seen some of the two thousand of their countrymen crucified by the Romans along the roadsides. They would have known some of the inhabitants of Sepphoris (a mere three miles north of Nazareth) who had been sold into slavery for aiding the insurrectionists' assault on the arsenal there. Some also would live to experience the horrors of the war against Rome in 66–70 c.e., one of the ghastliest in human history.

If the option "fight" had no appeal to them, their only alternative was "flight": passivity, submission, or, at best, a passive-aggressive recalcitrance in obeying commands. For them no third way existed. Submission or revolt spelled out the entire vocabulary of their alternatives to oppression.

Now we are in a better position to see why King James' faithful scholars translated *antistēnai* as "resist not." The king would not want people concluding that they had any recourse against his or any other sovereign's unjust policies. Therefore the populace must be made to believe that there are *two* alternatives and only two: flight or fight. Either we resist not or we resist. And Jesus commands us, according to these king's men, to resist not. Jesus appears to authorize monarchical absolutism. Submission is the will of God. And most modern translations have meekly followed in that path.

Is Gods will submissive for the people?

Neither of these alternatives has anything to do with what Jesus is proposing. It is important that we be utterly clear about this point before going on: *Jesus abhors both passivity and violence as responses to evil.* His is a third alternative not even touched by these options. A*ntistēnai* cannot be construed to mean submission.

Jesus clarifies his meaning by three brief examples. "If any one strikes you on the right cheek, turn to him the other also." Why the *right* cheek? How does one strike another on the right cheek anyway? Try it. A blow by the right fist in that right-handed world would land on the *left* cheek of the opponent. To strike the right cheek with the fist would require using the left hand, but in that society the left hand was used only for unclean tasks. Even to gesture with the left hand at Qumran carried the penalty of exclusion and ten days' penance (The Dead Sea Scrolls, 1QS 7). The only way one could strike the right cheek with the right hand would be with the *back of the right hand*. What we are dealing with here is unmistakably an insult, not a fistfight. The intention is not to injure but to humiliate, to put someone in his or her "place." One normally did not strike a peer thus, and if one did, the fine was exorbitant (4 zuz was the fine for a blow to a peer with a fist, 400 zuz for backhanding him; but to an underling, no penalty whatsoever—*Mishnah, Baba Qamma* 8:1-6). A backhand slap was the normal way of admonishing inferiors. Masters backhanded slaves; husbands, wives; parents, children; men, women; Romans, Jews. *We have here a set of unequal relations, in each of which retaliation would be suicidal.* The only normal response would be cowering submission.

It is important to ask who Jesus' audience is. In every case, Jesus' listeners are not those who strike, initiate lawsuits, or impose forced labor, but their victims ("If anyone strikes *you* . . . would sue *you* . . . forces *you* to go one mile . . ."). There are among his hearers people who were subjected to these very indignities, forced to stifle their inner outrage at the dehumanizing treatment meted out to them by the hierarchical system of caste and class, race and gender, age and status, and as a result of imperial occupation.

Why then does he counsel these already humiliated people to turn the other cheek? Because this action robs the oppressor of the power to humiliate. The person who turns the other cheek is saying, in effect, "Try again. Your first blow failed to achieve its intended effect. I deny you the power to humiliate me. I am a human being just like you. Your status does not alter that fact. You cannot demean me."

Such a response would create enormous difficulties for the striker. Purely logistically, what can he do? He cannot use the backhand because his nose is in the way. He can't use his left hand regardless. If he hits with a fist, he makes himself an equal, acknowledging the other as a peer. But the whole point of the back of the hand is to reinforce the caste system and its institutionalized inequality. Even if he orders the person flogged, the point has been irrevocably made. The oppressor has been forced, against his will, to regard this subordinate as an equal human being. The powerful person has been stripped of his power to dehumanize the other. This response, far from admonishing passivity and cowardice, is an act of defiance.

defying can be an act of non-violence.

The second example Jesus gives is set in a court of law. Someone is being sued for his outer garment.[8] Who would do that and under what circumstances? The Old Testament provides the clues.

> When you make your neighbor a loan of any sort, you shall not go into his house to fetch his pledge. You shall stand outside, and the man to whom you make the loan shall bring the pledge out to you. *And if he is a poor man,* you shall not sleep in his pledge; when the sun goes down, you shall restore to him the pledge that he may sleep in his cloak and bless you. . . . You shall not . . . take a widow's garment in pledge. (Deut. 24:10-13, 17)

Only the poorest of the poor would have nothing but an outer garment to give as collateral for a loan. Jewish law strictly required its return every evening at sunset, for that was all the poor had in which to sleep. The situation to which Jesus alludes is one with which all his hearers would have been all too familiar: the poor debtor has sunk ever deeper into poverty, the debt cannot be repaid, and his creditor has hauled him into court to try to seize his property by legal means.

Indebtedness was the most serious social problem in first-century Palestine. Jesus' parables are full of debtors struggling to salvage their lives. The situation was not, however, a natural calamity that had overtaken the incompetent. It was the direct consequence of Roman imperial policy. Emperors taxed the wealthy ruthlessly to fund their wars. Naturally, the rich sought non-liquid investments to secure their wealth. Land was best, but there was a problem: it was not bought and sold on the open market as today but was ancestrally owned and passed down over generations. Little land was ever for sale, in Palestine at least. Exorbitant interest, however, could be used to drive landowners into ever deeper debt until they were forced to sell their land. By the time of Jesus we see this process already far advanced: large estates (*latifundia*) owned by absentee landlords, managed by stewards, and worked by servants, sharecroppers, and day laborers. It is no accident that the first act of the Jewish revolutionaries in 66 C.E. was to burn the Temple treasury, where the record of debts was kept.

It is in this context that Jesus speaks. His hearers are the poor ("if any one would sue *you*"). They share a rankling hatred for a system that subjects them to humiliation by stripping them of their lands, their goods, and finally even their outer garments.

Why then does Jesus counsel them to give over their inner garment as well? This would mean stripping off all their clothing and marching out of court stark naked! Put yourself in the debtor's place, and imagine the chuckles this saying must have evoked. There stands the creditor, beet-red with embarrassment, your outer garment in one hand, your underwear in the other. You have suddenly turned the tables on him. You had no hope of winning the trial; the law was entirely in his favor. But you have refused to be humiliated, and at the same time

[handwritten margin note: give up everything so you don't have a way to be humiliated]

you have registered a stunning protest against a system that spawns such debt. You have said in effect, "You want my robe? Here, take everything! Now you've got all I have except my body. Is that what you'll take next?"

Nakedness was taboo in Judaism, and shame fell not on the naked party, but on the person viewing or causing one's nakedness (Gen. 9:20-27). By stripping you have brought the creditor under the same prohibition that led to the curse of Canaan. As you parade into the street, your friends and neighbors, startled, aghast, inquire what happened. You explain. They join your growing procession, which now resembles a victory parade. The entire system by which debtors are oppressed has been publicly unmasked. The creditor is revealed to be not a "respectable" moneylender but a party in the reduction of an entire social class to landlessness and destitution. This unmasking is not simply punitive, however; it offers the creditor a chance to see, perhaps for the first time in his life, what his practices cause, and to repent. Far from collaborating in injustice, the poor man has used the law, aikido-like, to make an exploitative law a laughing stock.

Jesus in effect is sponsoring clowning. In so doing he carries on a venerable tradition in Judaism. As a later saying of the Talmud runs, "If your neighbor calls you an ass, put a saddle on your back."[9]

The Powers That Be literally stand on their dignity. Nothing depotentiates them faster than deft lampooning. By refusing to be awed by their power, the powerless are emboldened to seize the initiative, even where structural change is not possible. This message, far from being a counsel of perfection unattainable in this life, is a practical, strategic measure for empowering the oppressed. It provides a hint of how to take on the entire system in a way that unmasks its essential cruelty and to burlesque its pretensions to justice, law, and order. Here is a poor man who will no longer be treated as a sponge to be squeezed dry by the rich. He accepts the laws as they stand, pushes them to the point of absurdity, and reveals them for what they really are. He strips nude, walks out before his compatriots, and leaves the creditor and the whole economic edifice he represents, stark naked.

Under the apartheid regime in South Africa, the authorities had for a long time sought a way to destroy a particular shantytown, without success. Then one day, after most of the men and women had left for work, the army arrived. The soldiers announced that the few women there had five minutes to gather their things and then the bulldozers would commence to work. The women, perhaps sensing the prudery of the farm boys who largely made up the army, stood in front of the bulldozers and stripped off all their clothes. The army fled.

Was Johan Stander, the renegade South African nationalist businessman, thinking of this passage, or was he just fed up, when he removed his trousers in front of the Port Elizabeth city hall in April 1986, while demonstrating against apartheid?[10]

Jesus' third example, the one about going the second mile, is drawn from the very enlightened practice of limiting the amount of forced labor that Roman soldiers could levy on subject peoples. Jews would have seldom encountered legionnaires except in time of war or insurrection. It would have been auxiliaries who were headquartered in Judea, paid at half the rate of legionnaires and rather a scruffy bunch. In Galilee, Herod Antipas maintained an army patterned after Rome's; presumably it also had the right to impose labor. Mile markers were placed regularly beside the highways. A soldier could impress a civilian to carry his pack one mile only; to force the civilian to go farther carried with it severe penalties under military law. In this way Rome attempted to limit the anger of the occupied people and still keep its armies on the move. Nevertheless, this levy was a bitter reminder to the Jews that they were a subject people even in the Promised Land.

To this proud but subjugated people Jesus does not counsel revolt. One does not "befriend" the soldier, draw him aside, and drive a knife into his ribs. Jesus was keenly aware of the futility of armed revolt against Roman imperial might and minced no words about it, though it must have cost him support from the revolutionary factions.

But why walk the second mile? Is this not to rebound to the opposite extreme: aiding and abetting the enemy? Not at all. The question here, as in the two previous instances, is how the oppressed can recover the initiative, how they can assert their human dignity in a situation that cannot for the time being be changed. The rules are Caesar's, but not how one responds to the rules—that is God's, and Caesar has no power over that.

Imagine then the soldier's surprise when, at the next mile marker, he reluctantly reaches to assume his pack (sixty-five to eighty-five pounds in full gear), and you say, "Oh no, let me carry it another mile." Why would you do that? What are you up to? Normally he has to coerce your kinsmen to carry his pack, and now you do it cheerfully and *will not stop!* Is this a provocation? Are you insulting his strength? Being kind? Trying to get him disciplined for seeming to make you go farther than you should? Are you planning to file a complaint? Create trouble?

From a situation of servile impressments, you have once more seized the initiative. You have taken back the power of choice. The soldier is thrown off-balance by being deprived of the predictability of your response. He has never dealt with such a problem before. Now you have forced him into making a decision for which nothing in his previous experience has prepared him. If he has enjoyed feeling superior to the vanquished, he will not enjoy it today. Imagine the hilarious situation of a Roman infantryman pleading with a Jew, "Aw, come on, please give me back my pack!" The humor of this scene may escape those who picture it through sanctimonious eyes, but it could scarcely have been lost on Jesus' hearers, who must have been regaled at the prospect of thus discomfiting their oppressors.

Some readers may object to the idea of discomfiting the soldier or embarrassing the creditor. But can people who are engaged in oppressive acts repent unless they are made uncomfortable with their actions? There is, admittedly, the danger of using nonviolence as a tactic of revenge and humiliation. There is also, at the opposite extreme, an equal danger of sentimentality and softness that confuses the uncompromising love of Jesus with being nice. Loving confrontation can free both the oppressed from docility and the oppressor from sin.

Even if nonviolent action does not immediately change the heart of the oppressor, it does affect those committed to it. As Martin Luther King Jr. attested, it gives them new self-respect and calls up resources of strength and courage they did not know they had. To those who have power, Jesus' advice to the powerless may seem paltry. But to those whose lifelong pattern has been to cringe, bow, and scrape before their masters, and who have internalized their role as inferiors, this small step is momentous. It is comparable to the attempt by black charwomen in South Africa to join together in what would be for some of them an almost insuperable step: to begin calling their employers by their first names.

These three examples amplify what Jesus means in his thesis statement: "Don't react violently against the one who is evil." Instead of the two options ingrained in us by millions of years of unreflective, brute response to biological threats from the environment—flight or fight—Jesus offers a third way. This new way marks a historic mutation in human development: the revolt against the principle of natural selection.[11] With Jesus a way emerges by which evil can be opposed without being mirrored:

Jesus' Third Way

- · Seize the moral initiative
- · Find a creative alternative to violence
- · Assert your own humanity and dignity as a person
- · Meet force with ridicule or humor
- · Break the cycle of humiliation
- · Refuse to submit or to accept the inferior position
- · Expose the injustice of the system
- · Take control of the power dynamic
- · Shame the oppressor into repentance

- Stand your ground
- Force the Powers to make decisions for which they are not prepared
- Recognize your own power
- Be willing to suffer rather than to retaliate
- Cause the oppressor to see you in a new light
- Deprive the oppressor of a situation where a show of force is effective
- Be willing to undergo the penalty for breaking unjust laws
- Die to fear of the old order and its rules

Flight	Fight
Submission	Armed revolt
Passivity	Violent rebellion
Withdrawal	Direct retaliation
Surrender	Revenge

It is too bad that Jesus did not provide fifteen or twenty further examples, since we do not tend toward this new response naturally. Some examples from political history might help engrave it more deeply in our minds.

In Alagamar, Brazil, a group of peasants organized a long-term struggle to preserve their lands against attempts at illegal expropriation by national and international firms (with the connivance of local politicians and the military). Some of the peasants were arrested and jailed in town. Their companions decided they were all equally responsible, so hundreds marched to town and filled the house of the judge, demanding to be jailed with those who had been arrested. The judge was finally obliged to send them all home, including the prisoners.[12]

Another, one that Jesus himself must have known and that may have served as a model for his examples: In 26 C.E., when Pontius Pilate brought the imperial standards into Jerusalem and displayed them at the Fortress Antonio overlooking the Temple, all Jerusalem was thrown into a tumult. These "effigies of Caesar that are called standards" not only infringed on the commandment against images but were the particular gods of the legions. Jewish leaders requested their removal. When Pilate refused, a large crowd of Jews "fell prostrate around his house and for five whole days and nights remained motionless in that position." On the sixth day, Pilate assembled the multitude in the stadium with the apparent intention of answering them. Instead, his soldiers surrounded the Jews in a ring three deep. As Josephus tells it,

> Pilate, after threatening to cut them down, if they refused to admit Caesar's images, signaled to the soldiers to draw their swords. Thereupon the Jews, as by concerted action, flung themselves in a body on the ground, extended their necks, and exclaimed that they were ready rather to die than to transgress the law. Overcome with astonishment at such intense religious zeal, Pilate gave orders for the immediate removal of the standards from Jerusalem.[13]

About 150 village women shut down most of a multinational oil company's operations in Nigeria for nearly a week. They commandeered a ChevronTexaco staff ferry to sneak into the company's

Escravos pipeline terminal. The unarmed women continued to occupy the terminal, stopping exports and trapping about 700 workers inside. The women wanted jobs for their sons and electricity in their impoverished homes in this, the world's sixth-largest oil exporter nation. When planes would land, the women would surround them so they couldn't take off again. Other teams of women shut down the docks and helicopter pads. Poorest of the poor, these mothers discovered the power of numbers, and, as of this writing, still had the upper hand (July 15, 2002, *New York Times,* A1).

Here is an example that deals with the perennial problem of bullying, as told by the mother in one of our workshops. Her son was the smallest kid in his class, and he was afflicted with chronic sinusitis. On his school bus there was a bully who was terrorizing all the kids. Finally, one day the boy had had it with the bully. He blew his nose into his right hand, then walked toward the bully, extending his hand, and saying, "I've always wanted to shake the hand of a real bully." The bully began to back up to the back of the bus, where he meekly sat down and never bothered anyone on that bus again, because that nose was always at the ready. What I like about this story is the way the boy used his weakness as a strength. Just as Jesus taught, he took the momentum of evil and used it to throw his opponent.

The nurses in a hospital in Saskatchewan were tired of being browbeaten, corrected in front of patients, and generally made to feel inferior by the doctors on staff. The nurses put their heads together and came up with a plan. They went to a sympathetic administration and set up a "pink alert," which would be transmitted over the intercom the next time a doctor started abusing a nurse. From all over the hospital, nurses who were free converged on the scene, surrounded the doctor, holding hands, and waited for him to make the first move. He located the smallest nurse and plunged toward her. But the circle merely gave with his charge. He tried another nurse; same result. It became like the childhood game Red Rover. The circle was like an amoeba that simply gave with his every move. Finally he dropped his hands, acquiescing in their lesson. That pretty much took care of that problem from then on out, for their circle, like the boy's nose, was ready at a moment's notice.

It is important to repeat such stories in order to extend our imaginations for creative nonviolence. Since it is not a natural response, we need to be schooled in it. We need models, and we need to rehearse it in our daily lives if we ever hope to resort to it in crises.

Sadly, Jesus' three examples have been turned into laws, with no reference to the utterly changed contexts in which they were being applied. His attempt to nerve the powerless to assert their humanity under inhuman conditions has been turned into a legalistic prohibition on schoolyard fistfights between peers. Pacifists and those who reject pacifism alike have tended to regard Jesus' infinitely malleable insights as iron rules, the one group urging that they be observed inflexibly, the other treating them as impossible demands intended to break us and catapult us into the arms of grace. The creative, ironic, playful quality of Jesus' teaching has thus been buried under an avalanche of humorless commentary. And as always, law kills.

How many a battered wife has been counseled, on the strength of a legalistic reading of this passage, to "turn the other cheek," when what she needs, according to the spirit of Jesus' words, is to find a way to restore her own dignity and end the vicious circle of humiliation, guilt, and bruising. She needs to assert some sort of control in the situation and force her husband to regard her as an equal, or get out of the relationship altogether. The victim needs to recover her self-worth and seize the initiative from her oppressor. And he needs to be helped to overcome his violence. The most creative and loving thing she could do, at least in the American setting, might be to have him arrested. "Turn the other cheek" is not intended as a legal requirement to be applied woodenly in every situation, but as the impetus for discovering creative alternatives that transcend the only two that we are conditioned to perceive: submission or violence, flight or fight.

Shortly after I was promoted from the "B" team to the varsity basketball squad in high school, I noticed that Ernie, the captain, was missing shot after shot from the corner because he was firing it like a bullet. So, helpfully I thought, I shouted, "Arch it, Ernie, arch it." His best friend, Ham, thought advice from a greenhorn impertinent, and from that day on verbally sniped at me without letup. I had been raised a Christian, so I "turned the other cheek." To each sarcastic jibe I answered with a smile or soft words. This confused Ham somewhat; by the end of the season he lost his taste for taunts.

It was not until four years later that I suddenly woke to the realization that I had not loved Ham into changing. The fact was, *I hated his guts*. It might have been far more creative for me to have challenged him to a fistfight. Then he would have had to deal with me as an equal. But I was *afraid* to fight him, though the fight would probably have been a draw. I was scared I might get hurt.

I was hiding behind the Christian "injunction" to "turn the other cheek," rather than asking, "What is the most creative, transformative response to this situation?" Perhaps I had done the right thing for the wrong reason, but I suspect that creative nonviolence can never be a genuinely moral response unless we are capable of first entertaining the possibility of violence and consciously saying "No." Otherwise our nonviolence may actually be a mask for cowardice, as it most certainly was for me.

The oppressed of the third world are justifiably suspicious that we of the first world are more concerned with avoiding violence than with realizing justice. Nobel Peace Prize laureate Adolfo Peréz Esquivel comments, "What has always caught my attention is the attitude of the peace movement in Europe and the United States, where nonviolence is envisioned as the final objective. Nonviolence is not the final objective. Nonviolence is a lifestyle. The final objective is humanity. It is life."[14]

For Discussion

1. What strikes you as new in this discussion of Jesus' teaching on nonviolence?

2. Were you taught to be cowardly by
the "doormat for Jesus" interpreta-
tion of this text?

3. If you have children, how might
you help them deal creatively with
bullying?

4. Do role-plays of Jesus' three examples
of nonviolence. You might plant
someone in the group who has on a
swimsuit or jogging shorts who can
play the role of the debtor.

Chapter 3

Perhaps it would help to juxtapose Jesus' teachings with Saul Alinsky's principles for nonviolent community action[15] so that we have a clearer sense of their practicality and pertinence to the struggles of our time. Among the rules Alinsky developed in his attempts to organize American workers and minority communities are these:

1. Power is not only what you have but what your enemy thinks you have.
2. Never go outside the experience of your people.
3. Wherever possible go outside the experience of the enemy.

Jesus recommended using one's experience of being belittled, insulted, or dispossessed (Alinsky's rule 2) in such a way as to seize the initiative from the oppressor, who finds the reaction of the oppressed totally outside his experience (second mile, stripping naked, turning the other cheek—rule 3) and forces him or her to believe in your power (rule 1) and perhaps even to recognize your humanity.

4. Make your enemies live up to their own book of rules.
5. Ridicule is your most potent weapon.
6. A good tactic is one that your people enjoy.
7. A tactic that drags on too long becomes a drag.

The debtor in Jesus' example turned the law against his creditor by obeying it (rule 4)—and throwing in his underwear as well. The ruthlessness of the creditor is thus used as the momentum by which to expose his rapacity (rule 5), and it is done quickly (rule 7) and in a way that could only regale the debtor's sympathizers (rule 6). All other such creditors are now put on notice, all other debtors armed with a new sense of possibilities.

8. Keep the pressure on.
9. The threat is usually more terrifying than the thing itself.
10. The major premise for tactics is the development of operations that will maintain a constant pressure upon the opposition.

Jesus, in the three brief examples he cites, does not lay out the basis of a sustained movement, but his ministry as a whole is a model of long-term social struggle (rules 8 and 10). Mark depicts Jesus movements as a *blitzkrieg.* "Immediately" appears eleven times in chapter one alone. Jesus' teaching poses an immediate threat to the authorities. The good he brings is misperceived as evil, his following is overestimated, his militancy is misread as sedition, and his proclamation of the coming Reign of God is mistaken as a manifesto for military revolution (rule 9). Disavowing violence, Jesus wades into the hostility of Jerusalem openhanded, setting simple truth against unequalled force. Terrified by the threat of this man and his following, the authorities resort to their ultimate deterrent, death, only to discover it impotent and themselves unmasked. The cross, hideous and macabre, becomes the symbol of liberation. The movement that should have died becomes a world religion.

11. If you push a negative hard and deep enough, it will break through to its counterside.
12. The price of a successful attack is a constructive alternative.
13. Pick the target, freeze it, personalize it, polarize it.

Alinsky delighted in using the most vicious behavior of his opponents—burglaries of movement headquarters, attempted blackmail, and failed assassinations—to destroy their public credibility. Here were elected officials, respected corporations, and trusted police engaging in patent illegalities in order to maintain privilege. In the same way, Jesus suggests amplifying an injustice (the other cheek, undergarment, second mile) in order to expose the fundamental wrongness of legalized oppression (rule 11). The law is "compassionate" in requiring that the debtor's cloak be

returned at sunset, yes; but Judaism in
its most lucid moments knew that the
whole system of usury and indebtedness
was itself the root of injustice and should
never have been condoned (Exod. 22:25).
The restriction of enforced labor to car-
rying the soldier's pack a single mile was
a great advance over unlimited impressments, but occupation troops had no
right to be on Jewish soil in the first
place. [Jesus' teaching is a kind of moral
jujitsu, a martial art for using the momentum of evil to throw it.] But it
requires penetrating beneath the con-
ventions of legality to issues of fundamental justice, and hanging onto them
with dogged persistence. As Gandhi put
it, "We are sunk so low that we fancy
that it is our duty and religion to do what
the law lays down." If people will only
realize that it is cowardly to obey laws
that are unjust, he continued, no one's
tyranny will enslave them.[16]

Picking the target, freezing it, person-
alizing it, and polarizing it are the means,
then, by which intensity is focused and
brought to bear (rule 13). For example,

infant formula merchants were discouraging breast feeding and promoting their product in countries where women could not afford the powder. Often the parents overdiluted the formula causing malnutrition, or mixed it with unsanitary water resulting in diarrhea and death. But you cannot fight all the merchants of infant formula in the third world at once; so you pick the biggest and most visible, Nestlé, even though doing so is technically unfair, since their competition gets off scot free. The focus pays off, however. Nestlé's recalcitrance leads to worldwide outrage and an international boycott. To avoid similar treatment most of the infant formula manufacturers make some changes. Eventually the boycott leader, the Infant Formula Action Coalition (INFACT), in conjunction with the World Health Organization and the United Nations International Children's Fund, draws up a code regulating the marketing of infant formula. In 1984, after eight years of struggle, Nestlé finally signs an agreement promising to comply with the new standards—which they promptly break. The boycott is continued until, this time, Nestlé complies. And the whole campaign has been instigated out of an office the size of a large closet.[17]

Jesus' constructive alternative (rule 12) was, of course, the Reign of God. Turning the tables on one's oppressor may be fun now and then, but long-term structural and spiritual change requires an alternative vision. As the means of purveying that vision and living it in the midst of the old order, Jesus established a new countercommunity that developed universalistic tendencies, erupting out of his own Jewish context and finally beyond the Roman Empire.

Jesus was not content merely to empower the powerless, however, and here his teachings fundamentally transcend Alinsky's. Jesus' sayings about nonretaliation are of one piece with his challenge to love our enemies. Here it is enough to remark that Jesus did not advocate nonviolence merely as a technique for outwitting the enemy, but as a just means of opposing the enemy in such a way as to hold open the possibility of the enemy's becoming just as well. Both sides must win. We are summoned to pray for our enemies' transformation, and to respond to ill-treatment with a love that not only is godly but also, I am convinced, can only be found in God.

To Alinsky's list I would like to add another "rule": Never adopt a strategy that you would not want your opponents to use against you. I would not object to my opponents using nonviolent direct actions against me, since such a move would require them to be committed to suffer and even die rather than resort to violence against me. It would mean that they would have to honor my humanity, believe that God can transform me, and treat me with dignity and respect. One of the ironies of nonviolence, in fact, is that those who depend on violent repression to defend their privileges *cannot* resort to nonviolence. There is something essentially contradictory between crushing the dissent of a society's victims and being willing to give one's life for justice and the truth.

While I was lecturing on nonviolence in South Korea, I had a chance to observe a "dance" between radical students and the police that took place every week. The students would march out of their dorms armed with rocks and Molotov cocktails, to face off police protected by shields. The students would hurl their projectiles, the police would hurl tear gas, and then they would all march away. To me it seemed an exercise in futility. One day, however, the police changed their tactics. When they encountered the students, they fell to the ground, blocking the street with their bodies. The students were nonplussed. You really can't throw Molotov cocktails at people who are lying down. So they marched back to the university campus with their weapons in their hands.

The following week the police reverted to form. Oppressors can imitate nonviolence for a short time, but their hearts are not in it. They are devotees of the Myth of Redemptive Violence. They believe in violence, and they feel naked and exposed without their weapons to attack and defend.

There are also particular tactics that, while technically nonviolent, would break the Golden Rule. I would not, for example, condone invading a party held for the children of top executives of a corporation that we oppose and throwing balloons filled with skunk-scented water, or paint-bombing the home of a nonsupportive bishop and slashing his tires, as one militant group of Christian activists did in the Pittsburgh area.[18]

Today we can draw on the cumulative historical experience of nonviolent social struggle over the centuries and employ newer tools for political and social analysis. But the spirit, the thrust, the surge for creative transformation that is the ultimate principle of the universe, is the same we see incarnated in Jesus. Freed from literalistic legalism, his teaching reads like a practical manual for empowering the powerless to seize the initiative even in situations impervious to change. It seems almost as if his teaching has only now, in this generation, become an inescapable task and practical necessity.

To people dispirited by the enormity of the injustices that crush us and the intractability of those in positions of power, Jesus' words beam hope across the centuries. We need not be afraid. We can reassert our human dignity. We can lay claim to the creative possibilities that are still ours, burlesque the injustice of unfair laws, and force evil out of hiding from behind the façade of legitimacy.

To risk confronting the Powers with such harlequinesque vulnerability, simultaneously affirming our own humanity and that of those whom we oppose, and daring to draw the sting of evil by absorbing it in our own bodies—such behavior is not likely to attract the faint of heart. But I am convinced that there is a whole host of people simply waiting for the Christian message to challenge them, for once, to a heroism worthy of their lives. Has Jesus not provided us with that word?

For Discussion

1. Are there times when nonviolence cannot be justified, when violence is the only solution?

2. Do you think Saul Alinsky is a helpful dialogue partner with Jesus, or is he too aggressive for your taste?

3. How far would you be willing to go in nonviolent direct action?

Chapter 4

Once we determine that Jesus' Third Way is not a perfectionistic avoidance of violence but a creative struggle to restore the humanity of all parties in a dispute, the legalism that has surrounded this issue becomes unnecessary. We cannot sit in judgment over the responses of others to their oppression. Gandhi continually reiterated that if a person could not act nonviolently in a situation, violence was preferable to submission. "Where there is only a choice between cowardice and violence, I would advise violence."[19] But Gandhi believed that a third way can always be found, if one is deeply committed to nonviolence.

Jesus' way, which is the way of the cross, means voluntarily taking on the violence of the Powers That Be, and that will mean casualties. But they will be nowhere near the scale that would result from violent revolution.

Britain's Indian colony of three hundred million people was liberated nonviolently at a cost of about eight thousand lives. The British apparently suffered not a single casualty, dead or wounded.[20] It took twenty-seven years (1919–46). France's Algerian colony of about ten million was liberated in seven years (1955–61) by violence, but it cost almost one million lives. The staggering differential in lives lost certainly cannot be ascribed to the French being more barbaric or determined to keep their colony than the British. And most of the French were fighting merely to keep a colony, *not* their native soil.

Solidarity in Poland nonviolently stood up to the ruthless power of a Communist government and lost about three hundred lives over a period of ten years. About the same time Argentina, in a violent but fruitless effort to take the Falkland/Malvinas Islands, lost approximately one thousand lives in two weeks against the British.

The armed revolt in Hungary was crushed by the Soviets at the cost of five to six thousand Hungarian lives; forty thousand were imprisoned, tortured or detained. In Czechoslovakia, where a spontaneous nonviolent resistance was mounted, seventy died, and political prisoners were *released.*

In the United States civil rights struggle, about fifty thousand demonstrators were jailed, but fewer than one hundred of those engaged in campaigns were killed. By contrast, armed revolutions in Cuba and Nicaragua cost twenty thousand lives each. In El Salvador, sixty thousand civilians died, quite apart from military casualties. Over the past thirty years one hundred thousand Guatemalans have lost their lives, out of a population of only 7.8 million. We cannot ignore the implications of these statistics, for *the comparative degree of carnage is a moral issue.*

We need to be very clear that it is in the interest of the Powers to make people believe that nonviolence doesn't work. To that end they create a double standard. If a single case can be shown where nonviolence doesn't work, nonviolence as a whole can then be discredited. No such rigorous standard is applied to violence, however, which regularly fails to achieve its goals. Close to two-thirds of all governments that assume power by means of coups d'état are ousted by the same means; only 1 in 20 post-coup governments give way to a civil government.[21]

The issue, however, is not just which *works* better, but also which *fails* better. While a nonviolent strategy also does not always "work" in terms of preset goals—though in another sense it always "works"—at least the casualties and destruction are far less severe.

I do not believe that the churches can adequately atone for their past inaction simply by baptizing revolutionary violence under the pretext of just war theory. No war today could be called just, given the inevitable level of casualties and atrocities.

Nonviolent revolutions sometimes happen by accident. They are usually more effective, however, when they are carefully prepared by grassroots training, discipline, organizing, and hard work. Training, because we need to know how to deal with police riots, how to develop creative strategies, how to defuse potentially violent eruptions. Discipline, because all too often agents provocateurs are planted in peace groups, whose task is to try to stir up violence. So we need to know how to neutralize people we suspect, by their actions, to be such agents. Organize, so as to create affinity groups that can act in concert, be able to identify by name every person in their cluster, and develop esprit de corps. And all that is hard work. But also (and this is a heavily guarded secret), nonviolent action in concert can be one of the most rewarding—and sometimes fun—activities available to human beings.

For Discussion

1. Granted that casualties are far less with nonviolence, why do people so often seem to prefer violence, even when nonviolence has been shown to be effective?

2. The Myth of Redemptive Violence seems to provide people with a sense of security. Why?
3. Which would give you a greater sense of security, to be in a stadium filled with people with weapons, or a stadium free of weapons?

Chapter 5

So far I have presented only pragmatic reasons for the use of nonviolence in political and social struggles. For the Christian, however, there are deeper and finally ultimate grounds for opting for Jesus' way.

1. The Love of Enemies

Jesus' Third Way bears at its very heart the love of enemies. This is the hardest word to utter in a context of conflict because it can so easily be misunderstood as spinelessness. But it is precisely the message King made central to his efforts in the polarized circumstances of the American South.

To our most bitter opponents we say: [We shall match your capacity to inflict suffering by our capacity to endure suffering.] We shall meet your physical force with soul force. Do to us what you will, and we shall continue to love you. We cannot in all good conscience obey your unjust laws, because nonco-operation with evil is as much a moral obligation as is cooperation with good. Throw us in jail, and we shall still love you. Bomb our homes and threaten our children, and we shall still love you. Send your hooded perpetrators of violence into our communities at the midnight hour and beat us and leave us half dead, and we shall still love you. [But be ye assured that we will wear you down by our capacity to suffer.] One day we shall win freedom, but not only for ourselves. We shall so appeal to your heart and conscience that we shall win *you* in the process, and our victory will be a double victory.[22]

It cannot be stressed too much: love of enemies has, for our time, become the litmus test of authentic Christian faith. Commitment to justice, liberation, or the overthrow of oppression is not enough, for all too often the means used have brought in their wake new injustices and oppressions. Love of enemies is the recognition that the enemy, too, is a child of God. The enemy too believes he or she is in the right, and fears us because we represent a threat against his or her values, lifestyle, or affluence. When we demonize our enemies, calling them names and identifying them with absolute evil, we deny that they have that of God within them that makes transformation possible. Instead, we play God. We write them out of the Book of Life. We conclude that our enemy has drifted beyond the redemptive hand of God.

I submit that the ultimate religious question today is no longer the Reformation's "How can I find a gracious God?" It is instead, "How can I find God in my enemy?" What guilt was for Luther, the enemy has become for us: the goad that can drive us to God. What has formerly been a purely private affair—justification by faith through grace—has now, in our age, grown to embrace the world. As John Stoner comments, we can no more save ourselves from our enemies than we can save ourselves from sin, but God's amazing grace offers to save us from both.[23] There is, in fact, no other way to God for our time but through the enemy, for loving the enemy has become the key both to human survival in the age of terror and to personal transformation. Either we find the God who causes the sun to rise on the evil and on the good, or we may have no more sunrises.

Of course it is difficult, even seemingly impossible, to forgive those who have killed members of your family, or tortured you, or sold out to the authorities. Yet this kind of behavior is nothing new. It is one of the rules of the power game that the oppressor always uses the maximum force possible within existing political and military constraints. It is little wonder then that people tend to feel that their own suffering is exceptional; it always is. Did not Jesus himself, and thousands of Christians all through the ages, experience the same? It is our very inability to love our enemies that throws us into the arms of grace. What law was for Luther, the enemy has become for us. It is precisely here, in the midst of persecution, that many will find themselves overtaken by the miraculous power of divine forgiveness. God's forgiving love can burst like a flare even in the night of our grief and hatred, and free us to love. It is in just such times as these, when forgiveness seems impossible, that the power of God most mightily manifests itself. There is a subtle pride in clinging to our hatreds as justified, as if our enemies had passed beyond even God's capacity to love and forgive, as if no one in human history had known sufferings as great as ours, as if Jesus' sufferings were inadequate and puny alongside what we must face.

To a certain extent the refusal to love enemies is a result of seeing the opposition as a monolith. We fail to note that the enemy camp is inevitably riddled with power struggles, fragmentation, back-stabbing, personal vendettas, bureaucratic infighting, and careerism, all of which conspire to prevent maximum efficiency in oppression. Likewise, we tend to freeze them in their current public postures, denying that they can make the very changes we are demanding of them. Many of them operate the governmental apparatus and therefore have a direct interest in the status quo. Unless these people are to be exterminated in a genocidal war or an endless guerrilla insurrection, they must be converted. And no one can show others the error that is within them, as Thomas Merton wisely remarked, unless the others are convinced that their critic first sees and loves the good that is within them.[24]

Love of enemies is, in the broadest sense, behaving out of one's own deepest self-interest: "that you may be sons and daughters of your Father who is in heaven" (Matt. 5:45). It is in my own self-interest to recognize that my opponents have jobs or mortgaged houses that tie them to the existing economic and political system. They are afraid they are losing their grip on the world. They need to be reassured that revolution will not strip them of all means of making a livelihood or all their hard-won security. Likewise, they need to be reassured continually that there will be a place for them in the new society being born.

We need to realize also the degree to which politicians refuse to change in order to save face, to avoid the appearance of backing down under pressure. For this reason, Gandhi always attempted to keep the demands of his campaigns specific to the local situation and to convince his opponents that the struggle was not for a victory over them but simply for fundamental justice. Once, having filled the jails over the right of untouchables to use the Nykom Temple Road, and finally securing their right to use it, Gandhi-led demonstrators refrained from using the road for a period of months. This provided the Brahmans and authorities a space in which to save face and back down without seeming to have capitulated. Gandhi distinguished between the "nonviolence of the weak," which uses harassment to break the opponent, and the "nonviolence of the strong" (what he called *satyagraha* or "truth force"), which seeks the opponent's good by freeing him or her from oppressive actions.[25]

King so imbued this understanding of nonviolence into his followers that it became the ethos of the entire civil rights movement. One evening, during the turbulent weeks when Selma, Alabama, was the focal point of civil right struggle, the large crowd of black and white activists standing outside the Ebenezer Baptist Church was electrified by the sudden arrival of a black funeral home operator from Montgomery. He reported that a group of black students demonstrating near the capitol just that afternoon had been surrounded by police on horseback, all escape barred, and cynically commanded to disperse or take the consequences. Then the mounted police waded into the students and beat them at will. Police prevented ambulances from reaching the injured for two hours. Our informant was the driver of one of those ambulances, and he had driven straight to Selma to tell us about it.

The crowd outside the church seethed with rage. Cries went up, "Let's march!" Behind us, across the street, stood, rank on rank, the Alabama State Troopers and the local police forces of Sheriff Jim Clark. The situation was explosive. A young black minister stepped to the microphone and said, "It's time we sang a song." He opened with the line, "Do you love Martin King?" to which those who knew the song responded, "Certainly, Lord!" "Do you love Martin King?" "Certainly, Lord!" "Do you love Martin King?" "Certainly, certainly, certainly Lord!" Right through the chain of command of the Southern Christian Leadership Conference he went, the crowd each time echoing, warming to the song, "Certainly, certainly, certainly Lord!" Without warning he sang out, "Do you love Jim Clark?"—the Sheriff?! "Cer . . . certainly, Lord" came the stunned, halting reply. "Do you love Jim Clark?" "Certainly, Lord"—it was stronger this time. "Do you love Jim Clark?" Now the point had sunk in, as surely as Amos' in chapters 1 and 2: "Certainly, certainly, certainly Lord!"

Rev. James Bevel then took the mike. We are not just fighting for our rights, he said, but for the good of the whole society. "It's not enough to defeat Jim Clark—do you hear me Jim?—we want you converted. We cannot win by hating our oppressors. We have to love them into changing."

And Jim Clark did change. When the voter registration drive in Selma was concluded, Jim Clark realized that he could not be re-elected without the black vote, so he began courting black voters. Later he even confessed, and I believe sincerely, that he had been wrong in his bias against blacks.

King enabled his followers to see the white racist also as a victim of the Principalities and Powers, in this case the whole ethos of the Southern Way of Life. Southern racists also needed to be changed. This provided a space and grace for transformation. While much more remains to be done in America than any of us likes to think, change has occurred, datable to events like these, when the tide of racial fury was channeled by the willingness of a few people to absorb its impact in their own bodies and to allow it to spread no farther.

An argument once heard in Latin America and South Africa is that while nonviolence is certainly the biblical norm, it can be used only against governments that have achieved a minimum moral level. It can work with the genial British in India but not with the violent defenders of apartheid or the brutal communists. This argument has been exploded by events, however, since the entire eastern bloc has collapsed under nonviolent pressure. As for the British in India, they were no more genial than the Romans in Palestine. Had Jesus waited for the Romans to achieve a minimum moral level, he never would have been able to articulate the message of nonviolence to begin with. On the contrary, his teaching does not presuppose a threshold of decency, but something of God in everyone. There is no one, and surely no entire people, in whom the image of God has been utterly extinguished. Faith in God means believing that *anyone* can be transformed, regardless of the past. To write off whole groups of people as intrinsically racist and violent is to accept the very same premise that upholds racist and oppressive regimes. That argument is used to support wholesale discrimination against blacks: blacks are not quite human, a different species altogether. The moment we argue that the South African defenders of apartheid are morally inferior beings, we reduce ourselves to their moral level. We become no different in kind than Nazis who claimed that Jews were racially inferior, or white supremacists in America who insist that blacks or Native Americans are animals or savages. As Narayan Desai remarks, "Nonviolence presupposes a level of humanness—however low it may be, in every human being."[26]

In the final analysis, then, love of enemies is trusting God for the miracle of divine forgiveness. If God can forgive, redeem, and transform me, I must also believe that God can work such wonders with anyone. Love of enemies is seeing one's oppressors through the prism of the Reign of God—not only as they now are but also as they can become: transformed by the power of God.

As Milan Machovec put it—and perhaps it took a Marxist who rediscovered Jesus to say it with such clarity:

The enemy must be resisted in so far as he serves the power of darkness, although it would be better to say that the power of darkness should be resisted rather than the enemy. He should be seen not as the servant of darkness but as someone who is capable of a future conversion. Therefore, though he uses evil means—despotism, the sword, force, darkness—one must not answer him with these same means. If one answered him in kind, with lies, deceit, violence and force, one would be denying oneself and him the future and the possibility of change, one would be perpetuating the kingdom of evil.[27]

2. The Means Are Commensurate with the New Order

Jesus' Third Way uses means commensurate with the new order we desire. Violent struggles are necessarily hierarchical; all warfare inevitably is. This pattern of centralized power-holding is not easily renounced after victory is won. After assuming power, ideological differences within the movement are dealt with by the same methods used to gain power: exterminations, purges, torture, and mass arrests. Revolutions must, in the nature of things, depend on men and women who have exercised their critical faculties. But insofar as the revolution's ideal is to create a society unanimous in its beliefs and wholly free from internal conflict, it must, if successful, destroy the very critical tendencies that made its success possible.

A reign of terror characterized the successful emergence to office of Stalin (Soviet Union), Mao (China), Bella (Algeria), Khomeini (Iran), and Pinochet (Chile). Stalin's attempts to control his real and imagined enemies led to the extermination of twenty million Soviet citizens—as many of them as were killed in World War II. In attempting to "protect the revolution," one Yugoslav commented, he "killed more good communists than the bourgeoisie of the whole world put together."[28] Even Castro arrested and left to rot those among his closest compatriots in the guerrilla struggle who dared to criticize his policies as prime minister. Such purges cost a new government its best leadership, lead to middle-class and professional flight, establish the security police at the heart of the nation's life, and undermine its recovery. Once the path of violence has been chosen, it cannot be easily renounced even in the new regime. In John Swomley's words, violence is "not conducive for teaching the respect for persons on which democracy depends."[29]

By contrast, nonviolent revolution is not a program for seizing power. It is, says Gandhi, a program for transforming relationships, ending in a peaceful transfer of power. When elements of the Indian Congress proposed resorting to violence on one occasion, Gandhi replied, "We've come a long way with the British. When they eventually leave we want them to do so as friends."[30] This attitude of respect for the opponent requires keeping the dialogue open. That demands courage. It also helps reduce the paranoia that builds from being under continual surveillance. Upon his release from detainment in 1985, Richard Steele, an organizer of the End Conscription Campaign in apartheid South

Africa, continued to be followed by his interrogators. They would be parked outside his apartment every morning. Instead of ignoring them or trying to shake them off his tail, he made it a practice to go over and speak with them. This made them very nervous. Their explicit purpose was intimidation, and now they were forced to speak to this man who refused to be cowed. By insisting on treating them as human beings, he was challenging them to become who they will be in the Reign of God.

Violence simply is not radical enough, since it generally changes only the rulers but not the rules. What use is a revolution that fails to address the fundamental problem: the existence of domination in all its forms, and the myth of redemptive violence that perpetuates it?

3. Respect for the Rule of Law

Jesus' Third Way preserves respect for the rule of law even in the act of resisting oppressive laws. Violent revolutionaries are involved in a contradiction that jeopardizes the very order they wish to establish. They plan to gain power by the very means that they will declare illegal when they gain power. But they will have established a precedent that legitimates the use of violence by those who disagree with them and wish to replace them. Since they will not have fostered democracy in their rise to power, they can only resort to force in silencing their opposition.

King's insight was that blacks, if they wished to achieve a share of the American Dream, could not begin by destroying the institutions and violating that respect for law that were the source of the benefits they sought. We want a society freed from every last vestige of injustice, but at the same time we also want a society where people still stop for traffic lights, where robbers are apprehended, and where gangs of lawless ruffians are not free to roam the streets. In the civil disobedience practiced by King and Gandhi, a person in the very act of appealing to a higher moral authority subjects himself or herself to the principle of civil law. No proponent of Jesus' Third Way would ever attempt to get off scot-free for breaking an unjust law, for that would encourage the chaos of lawlessness in a society already rendered intolerable by legalized injustices. Civil disobedience always must be engaged in with deep respect for the idea of law. Indeed, it is voluntary submission to the due penalty of the law that discourages frivolous violations.

Citing Romans 13:1-7 and its call for "every person [to] be subject to the governing authorities" does not imply blind obedience. Submission may lead to obedience but does not necessarily require it. Jesus was depicted as subject to his parents (Luke 2:51), but he also refused to obey his own mother's command (see also Mark 3:31-35). All things are subjected to Christ (Eph. 1:20-22), but they do not yet all obey him. Jesus subjected himself to Jewish law, yet he deliberately broke it where it violated his discernment of God's will. Yet he whom the church would later declare greater than the law submitted to its penalties for his disobedience. So too Peter and John stated before the Sanhedrin, "Whether it is right in the sight of God to listen to you rather than to God, you must judge; for we cannot but speak of what we have seen and heard" (Acts 4:19).

Second, Romans 13:2 has been translated in such a way that all resistance even to the most satanic despotism appears to be prohibited. The Revised Standard Version is representative: "Therefore he who resists the authorities resists what God has appointed, and those who resist will incur judgment." The first term for "resist," *antitassō,* is a military term meaning literally "to range in battle against," "to post in adverse array, as an army," "to set oneself in armed opposition." The second and third instances of "resist" in the same sentence are our old friend from Matthew 5:39, *anthistēmi.* It too indicates armed insurrection, violent resistance. Romans 13:1-7 is not, then, an injunction against all forms of resistance to an unjust regime, but only *armed* resistance. Romans 13:2 might then be translated, "Therefore the person who engages in armed revolt against the political system commits insurrection against what God has ordained." God wills that there be political order and not chaos. Human life is intolerable apart from the rule of law.

Third, this rule is to be for the benefit of all. The ruler "is God's servant for your good" (Rom. 13:4). What happens when that rule is no longer good for the majority of the people? Romans 13 only tells us how government *ought* to be, as Allan Boesak reminds us. Revelation 13 tells us how government ought *not* to be. "The servant of God can very easily become the beast."[31] Even when the government is in a state of apostasy and rebellion against God, however, the Christian is still encouraged to struggle against it nonviolently (Rev. 13:10).

We too should, following Jesus, refuse ever to obey an unjust law. But by undergoing its recoil against us, we affirm our willingness to suffer on behalf of a higher law that we are determined to see transform the law of the land. We are lawful in our illegality. It is only because we submit to the principle of law that we demand that unjust laws be made just in the first place.

Even when the Powers That Be are repressive in the extreme, they still embody something that must be honored and to which we must subject ourselves: the *principle* of law. Romans 13, however misused by oppressors, articulates this fundamental truth. We must begin from a basis of legality in order to foster a new society that will abide by the letter and the spirit of just laws.

4. Rooting Out the Violence

Jesus' Third Way requires us to root out the violence within our own souls. To resist something, we must meet it with counterforce. If we resist violence with violence, we simply mirror its evil. We become what we resist. But even when we resist evil creatively, seizing the initiative and lovingly challenging the Powers to change, there is danger.

The easiest temptation to unmask is self-righteousness. What a wonderfully expansive feeling it is to denounce evil grandly! What a host of oversights and sins are covered by such greasy goodness, how nice we feel about ourselves. In such a mood it is easy to fall into us/them thinking, to forget our own complicity in our past complacency toward the evil we now so tardily (always, it seems, tardily) oppose. During such seizures of summer saintliness it is virtually impossible not to demonize the enemy; indeed, part of the payoff of demonizing others is to feel good about ourselves.

Every outer evil inevitably attracts from our own depths parts of ourselves that resemble it. To engage evil is therefore a spiritual act, because it will require of us the rare courage to face our own most ancient and intractable evils within. It means abandoning one of the greatest and oldest lies: that the world is made up of good people and bad people. There is a double movement of psychic energy. We identify someone else as evil and unconsciously project our own evil onto that person. But the person or system that we call enemy also evokes the evil within, like a piano string set vibrating by a piercing scream. This two-way traffic of projection and introjection, if not halted, eventually becomes a form of mimesis, where each party begins to imitate the other.

What is so very painful in the spiritual discipline required to face this inner darkness is that some of it may not be redeemable. I would like to become nonviolent from the heart, but there is a killer, a torturer, a coward, and a dictator in me that would like to keep me in psychic detention forever. Call it Satan, the shadow, the dark side of God, whatever, it is a brute fact documented down through the history of the human race. Something there is in me that does not want to be redeemed, or see others freed as well. I believe this fact is universal.

Christian theology calls it the fall or original sin. Judaism knows it as the evil impulse. Even recognizing that this aspect is in me does not free me of its power. I must bring a great deal of consciousness and forgiving love to bear on these parts of me in order to limit their damage. I must continually offer them up to God for whatever healing and transformation is possible. People who engage in nonviolent protest without at least some awareness of this cesspool of violence within them can actually jeopardize the lives of their compatriots. In a protest against bombing, they themselves become the bomb, and explode.

It is hard enough getting people to engage in Jesus' way of resistance to evil. Then we tell them they have to go through an arduous spiritual discipline to neutralize the oppressor within! As Shelley Douglass puts it, we do not want to have to change our lives to bring about justice. The hardest moment comes when our own internal oppressor meets the outside reality that it supports. It is not out there, but in me, that the oppressor must die.[32]

For most people this may be asking too much. They prefer the heady, extroverted phase of action. But Jesus' way has built into it an uncanny solution. It lands many of its practitioners in jail. That is where Paul did must of his meditating, thinking, and writing, and Gandhi and King as well. South African opponent of apartheid Beyers Naude says that the best thing that ever happened to him was his banning. Strange, wry providence, that prison should have been, for so many, not the unfortunate price of protest, but the gracious, fiery crucible that, as one black labor organizer told us, "killed my fear and made me all the more determined to struggle for liberation, to death if necessary"–not said with bravado, but with a quiet, serene smile.

5. Not a Law but a Gift

Jesus' Third Way is not a law but a gift. It establishes us in freedom, not necessity. It is something we are not required to do, but enabled to do. It is a "Thou mayest," not a "Thou must." It is not something we do in order to secure our own righteousness before God. It is rather something that we are made capable of when we know that the power of God is greater than the powers of death.

Much as I fantasize about violence toward my enemies, I cannot conceive of actually killing them. Yet even if I am committed to nonviolence, I may find myself in a situation where I am not able to find a creative, third way, and must choose between the lesser of two violences, two guilts. Even then, however, it is not a question of justifying the violence. I simply must, as Bonhoeffer did, take on myself the guilt and cast myself on the mercy of God.[33] But in a situation of extreme oppression, it is far better that we act violently than let our fear of sin and guilt paralyze us into no act at all. I cannot even be sure that my nonviolent acts are just, or right, or willed by God.

Nor can we condemn those who in desperation resort to counter-violence against the massive violence of an unjust order. We should not strike a neutral pose, says John Swomley, but side with the oppressed, even if they follow the bad example of their oppressors in resorting to violence. "I wanted the oppressed Hungarians to gain their freedom from the Soviet Union in 1956," he writes, "even though they used violence."[34] Violence is not an absolute evil to be avoided at all costs. It is not even the main problem, but only the presenting symptom of an unjust society. And peace is not the highest good; it is rather the outcome of a just social order.

The Nicaraguan revolution has often been cited as an example where violence "worked," as it indeed did—at the cost of twenty thousand lives. But violent revolt there was not inevitable. Miguel D'Escoto, free Nicaragua's foreign minister and a Roman Catholic priest, tells why.

Eight years before the insurrection, after the earthquake, I talked to the archbishop. And I said, "Archbishop, don't you see how this is going to explode?" To me it seemed inevitable that sooner or later in spite of the great patience of our people—everything human is limited—that patience would run out. I said, "Bishop, it is going to be terrible, there will be so many dead people, so much destruction and death. Why don't we go into the streets? You lead us, armed with the rosary in our hands and prayers on our lips and chants and songs in repudiation for what has been done to our people. The worst than can happen to us is the best, to share with Christ the cross if they shoot us.

"If they do shoot us, there will be a consciousness aroused internationally. And maybe the people in the United States will be alerted and will pressure their government so that it won't support Somoza, and then maybe we can be freed without the destruction that I see ahead."

And the archbishop said, "No Miguel, you tend to be a little bit idealistic, and this destruction is not going to happen." And then when it did happen, the church insisted on nonviolence.

To be very frank with you, I don't think that violence is Christian. Some may say that this is a reactionary position. But I think that the very essence of Christianity is the cross. It is through the cross that we will change.

I have come to believe that creative nonviolence has to be a constitutive element of evangelization and of the proclamation of the gospel. But in Nicaragua nonviolence was never included in the process of evangelization.

The cancer of oppression and injustice and crime and exploitation was allowed to grow, and finally the people had to fight with the means available to them, the only means that people have found from of old: armed struggle. Then the church arrogantly said violence was bad, nonviolence was the correct way.

I don't believe that nonviolence is something you can arrive at rationally. We can develop it as a spirituality and can obtain the grace necessary to practice it, but not as a result of reason. Not that it is anti-reason, but that it is not natural. The natural thing to do when somebody hits you is to hit them back.

We are called upon to be supernatural. We reach that way of being, not as a result of nature, but of prayer. But that spirituality and prayer and work with people's consciences has never been done. We have no right to hope to harvest what we have not sown.[35]

The counterviolence of the oppressed may even in the mystery of God's wrath be something that God is able to employ. Just as God used Assyrian military conquest as the rod to punish Israel for its apostasy (Isa. 10:5), so the violence of the poor has awakened some people to the severity of their poverty. So while I do not believe that Christians have a vo-

cation for violence, and should actively
oppose its use, we are also not permitted
to sit in judgment over those who resort
to violence. God can take care of that.

6. The Way of the Cross

Jesus' Third Way is the way of the cross.
The cross was not just Jesus' identification with the victims of oppression; it
was, as Rob Robertson remarks, also his
way of dealing with these evils. It was not
because he was a failed insurrectionist
that Jesus died as he did, but because he
preferred to suffer injustice and violence
rather than be their cause.[36] Following
the Philippines' successful nonviolent
revolution, Bishop Francisco Claver, S.J.,
wrote, "We choose nonviolence not
merely as a strategy for the attaining of
the ends of justice, casting it aside if it
does not work. We choose it as an end in
itself . . . because we believe it is the way
Christ himself struggled for justice."[37]

The cross means that death is not the
greatest evil one can suffer. It means that

I am free to act faithfully without undo regard for the outcome. God can bring out of voluntarily assumed suffering the precious seeds of a new reality. I cannot really be open to the call of God in a situation of oppression if the one thing I have excluded as an option is my own suffering and death.

Jesus' Third Way is not natural. We have not been prepared for it through millions of years of conditioning for flight or fight responses. We do not come to these things by virtue of a sunny disposition but by conversion, practice, imagination, and risk. Nonviolent training needs to become a regular and repetitive component of every change-oriented group's life; it is not a last minute strategy that can be donned at will like an asbestos suit.

The cross also means not necessarily winning. The Principalities and Powers are so colossal, entrenched, and determined that the odds for their overthrow or repentance are minuscule, whatever means we use. It is precisely because the outcome is in question, however, that we need to choose a way of living that already is a living of the outcome we desire. The Reign of God is already in the process of arriving when we choose means consistent with its arrival. So for Gandhi the question, after one, two, three decades of struggle, was never: Shall we abandon *satyagraha* for violence? That would have been like asking, Shall I give up my integrity for the sake of the truth?

There is a horrible, yet I am afraid, absolutely accurate vision in Revelation 6:9-11, at the opening of the fifth seal:

> When he opened the fifth seal, I saw under the altar the souls of those who had been slaughtered for the word of God and for the testimony they had given; they cried out with a loud voice, "Sovereign Lord, holy and true, how long will it be before you judge and avenge our blood on the inhabitants of the earth?" They were each given a white robe and told to rest a little longer, until the number would be complete both of their fellow

servants and of their brothers and sisters, who were soon to be killed as they themselves had been killed.

There are times and places where suffering and even death become inescapable. More Christians were martyred in the twentieth century than in all the previous years since the founding of the church *combined.* Jesus' Third Way was certainly no way to avoid persecution and death. On the contrary, Jesus' way deliberately evokes the violence of an oppressive system, using its momentum to throw it. As Charles Williams remarked, if the energy of evil is to be deflected or transformed, something or someone must suffer its impact.

And yet we must not allow a theology of the cross to lock us into a rationalization for failure. No one believed South Africa could be transformed without violence, or that the Berlin Wall would come crashing down without a fight. The power of the Holy Spirit is a constant challenge to transcend the present order and to win the victories, large and small, that are actually possible.

The cross requires courage. During the vigilante torching of Crossroads/KTC, in the Cape Town section of South Africa, on June 9–11, 1986, John Freeth, an Anglican priest, moved back and forth under fire between the vigilantes and their victims, helping the wounded, comforting the dying, trying to get the police to stop the carnage. He noticed that many of the black vigilantes looked down or away when he encountered them, as if they felt ashamed for what they were doing. It occurred to him that if he could only find twenty-five clergy willing to make a human chain between the opposing black factions, that it would give those vigilantes who had been recruited against their wishes a face-saving way to back off. The moral force of the act and the public exposure it involved would make it hard for the instigators to press the attack. It also would unmask police support for the attacking vigilantes and give the lie to their bogus claims that they were attempting to prevent violence.

A capital idea, I said by phone from the United States. Can you find twenty-five? "Twenty-five?" he laughed. "So far I've had difficulty finding two and a half!

Most think I'm a bit potty." Did he just not know whom to call? Or did they know so little of the history of nonviolent interventions that this tested and often successful tactic appeared to them bizarre? Or was it—I hesitate to put it so baldly, but someone must—a case of sheer cowardice?

Or was it a bit of all three, abetted by an even more significant factor: the lack of a structure for summoning and empowering people to transcend their perfectly natural and prudent fear? Prior to undergoing nonviolence training in Selma in 1965, I was shaking in my socks. But fear is remarkably responsive to the Holy Spirit. Our anxiety need not remain in our path, blocking our obedience; we can put it behind us, where it continues to whimper but no longer determines our deeds.

Daniel Berrigan observes that most people find it more sane to contemplate nuclear suicide than civil disobedience. Millions march off willingly to wars, fortified by blind trust in chance: the unexpressed hope that it will be their buddies who get it, not they themselves, and that they will kill the enemy, not be killed. It takes far more courage to walk into a situation voluntarily, knowing that suffering is inevitable, choosing to draw the poison of that violence with one's own body rather than perpetuating the downward spiral of hate. But that is what we celebrate in every Eucharist as Jesus' way. Will it not be ours as well?

For Discussion

1. How is it possible to love our enemies? Isn't an enemy by definition someone whom we can't love?
2. Share stories about times when you forgave or were forgiven.
3. Write a dialogue between you and someone from whom you are presently estranged, with the intent of being reconciled.
4. Since September 11, 2001, many previously nonviolent people feel threatened by terrorists and are willing to use whatever means necessary to wipe them out. What have your feelings been about using violence since those and other recent terrorist attacks?

5. Why do the means determine the end?
   Why can't we use violence to free us
   from violence?

6. If laws are unjust, why should we
   have to obey them? Why not just
   declare them wrong and ignore them?

7. Some activists become so exhausted
   from struggling against the Powers
   that they are forced to turn inward to
   find new resources for the long haul.
   Others who are spiritual seekers find
   themselves thrust toward social struggle as a result of their inner reflections. Do either of these fit you?
   How? How not?

8. Camus wrote: "There is merely bad
   luck in not being loved; there is tragedy in not loving. All of us, today, are
   dying of this tragedy.
   For violence and hatred dry up the
   heart itself; the long fight for justice
   exhausts the love that nevertheless
   gave birth to it. In the clamor in
   which we live, love is impossible and
   justice does not suffice."[38] Comment.

9. Can you identify ways and places that the Holy Spirit can be seen transforming the world, however small?

10. Can you identify ways and places that the Holy Spirit has seemingly let you down in your face-offs with the Powers?

Chapter 6

One key to the success of the non-violent victory in the Philippines was the degree of participation by the churches' top leadership in nonviolence training. A year and a half before Marcos was toppled from power, Jean and Hildegard Goss-Mayr of the International Fellowship of Reconciliation were invited by Filipino Christians to come to the Philippines to hold seminars on the gospel and active nonviolence. These seminars lasted six weeks and included one with thirty Roman Catholic bishops. Richard Deats, with the American Fellowship of Reconciliation, followed with three weeks of training, primarily for Protestants. Out of these seminars a group of Filipinos founded AKKAPKA ("Action for Peace and Justice"). Within the year AKKAPKA, under the leadership of Fr. Jose Blanco and Tess Ramiro, held forty nonviolence seminars in thirty provinces, with the co-operation of many Filipino bishops, clergy, nuns, and lay leaders. At strategy sessions, which regularly included Cory Aquino and Cardinal Sin, various scenarios for protecting against election fraud were discussed. When the crisis came, AKKAPKA and other organizations had trained *half a million poll watchers* who were prepared to give their lives to prevent falsification of ballots.

Later, when key military leaders defected to a "rebel" army base, Cardinal Sin went to three orders of contemplative nuns and told them, "We are now in battle. Prostrate yourselves, pray and fast. You are the powerhouse of God and central to the battle. Fast until death if necessary." Then, over the Catholic radio, Cardinal Sin called upon the people to place their unarmed bodies between the defectors and the government troops. There were only a few in the beginning, but soon hundreds of thousands of people made a human wall around the base, tying yellow ribbons on the gun barrels of tanks and offering soldiers gifts of food, candies, and garlands of flowers. President Marcos ordered the tanks to attack. Their commanders refused to proceed when nuns and priests sat in front of their tracks. Pilots, ordered to bomb the rebel base with its human cordon, refused and defected to a nearby United States military base.[39]

There were other factors in the success of nonviolence in the Philippines. Bishop Francisco Claver, S.J., was tireless in holding up the relation of nonviolence to the gospel year after year. Ninoy Aquino converted to nonviolence in prison, where he studied violent, third-world revolutions and came in the end to feel that Gandhi, rather than Mao and others, was his mentor. He returned from exile armed only with "faith and determination." After he was murdered as he descended from his plane, his wife Cory took up his fallen banner. Sadly, that revolution was all too quickly co-opted by the wealthy class, and a great opportunity for justice turned into flat disappointment.

Nevertheless, there were signs of hope. No one could have predicted the defection of the Filipino defense minister and the military chief of staff. No one could have dared dream that civilians would succeed in nonviolently stopping planes and tanks by surrounding the rebel base. ("This is something new," exclaimed one of the defectors, Colonel Alimonte. "Soldiers are supposed to protect the civilians. In this particular case, you have civilians protecting the soldiers."[40])

The debate about violence versus non-violence today is simply no longer fruitful. Nonviolent acts of civil disobedience, protest and confrontation are, for many people, the only effective actions possible. And let no one say, "But the government will never allow it." The government does not allow violence either. The oppressed and their allies simply are no longer asking what the government allows. They are fostering what Jonathan Schell calls "an epidemic of freedom in a closed society"[41] by ignoring official permissions and living "as if" the new society were at hand. Increased governmental controls will not be the occasion for abandoning nonviolence. They will simply make it costlier.

It is not unusual in a protracted struggle to experience bewilderment and even despair after each new measure taken by the Powers to crush rising opposition. That experience is not only characteristic, but a necessary precondition of creative response. Creativity is always the improbable grasped out of the teeth of despair. The allure of violence at such times is understandable. It does not require the same degree of imagination and invention.

Our time has witnessed the emergence of a new historical phenomenon: the National Security State, a colossus of surveillance and repressive might made virtually impregnable as a result of the wizardry of military and electronic technology. Such a colossus should deprive us of all hope. But the paradoxical consequence is just the opposite. Since armed resistance is largely futile, people have taken recourse in nonviolent means. Non-violence has even become the preferred method of people who have never contemplated absolute pacifism. Because leaders are arrested almost as soon as they emerge, resistance groups have innovated nonhierarchical and democratic organizational forms. Means and ends coalesce as people create for themselves social instruments for change that already embody the better life they seek ahead. For this reason it seems to me that those who have held back from throwing the full weight of moral authority into a nonviolent mode of struggle need do so no longer. The question is not pacifism, but a more effective, united struggle for goals shared by all. There would not even be the need for people to reach theoretical agreement on nonviolence as a total philosophy, as long as they were agreed that in specific campaigns they would remain nonviolent.

Many people have not aspired to Jesus' Third Way because it has been presented to them as absolute pacifism, a life-commitment to nonviolence in principle, with no exceptions. They are neither sure that they can hold fast to its principles in every situation nor sure that they have the saintliness to overcome their own inner violence. Perhaps a more traditional Christian approach would make more sense. We know that nonviolence is the New Testament pattern. We can commit ourselves to following Jesus' way as best we can. We know we are weak and will probably fail. But we also know that God loves and forgives us and sets us back on our feet after every failure and defeat.

Seen in this light, Jesus' Third Way is not an insuperable counsel to perfection attainable only by the few. It is simply the right way to live, and can be pursued by many. The more who attempt it, the more mutual support there will be in following it.

Notes

1. Ronald J. Sider and Richard K. Taylor, *Nuclear Holocaust and Christian Hope* (Downers Grove, Ill.: InterVarsity, 1982), 250–51.

2. Gene Sharp, *The Politics of Nonviolent Action*, Extending Horizons Books (Boston: Sargent, 1973), 117–434. See also Sider and Taylor, *Nuclear Holocaust*, 236–87.

3. "Resistance to evil by peaceful means" is an accurate rendition of *satyagraha*, but it is confusing, since the means King and Gandhi chose often deliberately provoked conflict and shattered a bogus "peace" masking systemic or legalized violence. The Brazilians have found a nice phrase in *firmeza permanente*, "relentless firmness," which is an excellent translation for the New Testament virtue of *hupomonē*. Luke 21:12-19, for example, predicts that the faithful "will be brought before synagogues and put in prison; you will be haled before kings

and governors for your allegiance to me. . . .
Even your parents and brothers, your relations and friends, will betray you. Some of
you will be put to death. . . . By *standing firm*
(*hupomonē*) you will win true life for yourselves" (NEB). The term connotes "endurance,
obstinacy, power to sustain blows, fortitude,
perseverance, steadfastness"—relentless firmness quite ably catches the meaning. One
definition of *satyagraha* also coincides with
hupomonē: "power which comes through a
tenacious devotion to the ultimate reality"
(William Robert Miller, *Nonviolence* [New
York: Schocken, 1972], 28). This quality of
absolute intransigence is an indispensable
characteristic of Christian existence in the
Book of Revelation (1:9; 2:2, 3, 19; 3:10;
13:10; 14:12). Its anemic rendition as "patient
endurance" in the RSV and NRSV empties it of
its political impact.

4. In April 1986, the South African magazine
Praxis ran a poem by Cecil Rajendra that tells
the heart-rending story of a poor man who
decides to kill his starving family and himself
rather than suffer any longer. At the end the
poet asks the reader, "Do you still believe in
non-violence?" Rajendra completely misiden-
tifies nonviolence with submission and the ac-
ceptance of injustice.

5. Cited by John W. de Gruchy, *Bonhoeffer and South Africa* (Grand Rapids: Eerdmans, 1984), 98.

6. Miller, *Nonviolence,* 51.

7. *Anthistēmi* is the Greek word most frequently used in the Septuagint to translate the Hebrew *qum.* Forty-four out of seventy-one times it carries the sense of "to rise up" against someone in revolt or war. *A Greek-English Lexicon* (Henry George Liddell, and Robert Scott, eds. New York: Oxford University Press, 1996) defines it as "to set against, especially in battle." We can be virtually assured that it is used in Matthew 5:39 in the sense of "to resist forcibly" because the Jesus tradition elsewhere cites Micah 7:6—"For the son treats the father with contempt, the daughter *rises up* against her mother, the daughter-in-law against her mother-in-law; your enemies are members of your own household" (see Matt. 10:34-36; Luke 12:53). And Jesus may have formulated the statement about debtors giving their clothing to creditors in contrast to Habakkuk 2:7, where the wealthy are threatened with visions of debtors suddenly *rising up* in bloody revolt.

8. Matthew and Luke are at odds on whether it is the outer garment (Luke) or the inner garment (Matthew) that is being taken. But the Jewish practice of giving the outer garment as

collateral for a loan makes it clear that Luke is correct.

9. *Babylonian Talmud, Baba Qamma* 92b.

10. *Weekly Mail*, South Africa (April 25–May 1, 1986), 5.

11. Gerd Theissen, *Biblical Faith: An Evolutionary Approach,* trans. John Bowden (Philadelphia: Fortress Press, 1985), 122.

12. *Essays on Nonviolence,* ed. Thérèse de Coninck (Nyack, N.Y.: Fellowship of Reconciliation, n.d.), 38.

13. Josephus, *War* 2.172-74; *Antiquities* 18.55-59. Despite the similarity to a wolf's baring his throat to show he is overmastered, the two acts are polar opposites. The wolf is surrendering; these Jews were being defiant. The wolf seeks to save its life; these Jews were prepared to die for their faith. The Jews later tried the same tactic against the Emperor Gaius (Caligula), and again prevailed, aided by the providential death of the emperor (*Antiquities* 18.257-309).

14. "An Interview with Adolfo Peréz Esquivel," *Fellowship* 51 (July/August, 1985): 10.

15. Saul Alinsky, *Rules for Radicals* (New York: Random House, 1971).

16. Gandhi, *The Science of Satyagraha,* ed. Anand T. Hingorani (Bombay: Bharatiya Vidya Bhanan, 1970), 67.

17. Conversations with Doug Johnson and Elaine Lamy of INFACT.

18. "Prophets in Steeltown," *Christian Century* (May 8, 1985): 460–62.

19. Gandhi consistently turned away those who were fearful of taking up arms or felt themselves incapable of violent resistance. "Non-violence cannot be taught to a person who fears to die and has no power of resistance." "He who has not overcome fear cannot practice *ahimsa* [the resolve not to hurt a living being] to perfection." "At every meeting I repeated the warning that unless they felt that in non-violence they had come into possession of a force infinitely superior to the one they had and in the use of which they were adept, they should have nothing to do with non-violence and resume the arms they had possessed before" (cited by Joan V. Bondurant, *Conquest of Violence* [Princeton: Princeton University Press, 1958], 28–29, 139).

20. John W. Swomley Jr., *Liberation Ethics* (New York: Macmillan, 1972), 172. On Solidarity, see the exceptional article by Jonathan Schell: "Reflections: A Better Today," *New Yorker* (February 3, 1986): 47–67.

21. Miles D. Wolpin, *Militarism and Social Revolution in the Third World* (Totowa, N.J.: Allanheld, Osmun, 1981), 3.

22. Martin Luther King Jr., sermon delivered at Dexter Avenue Baptist Church in Montgomery, Alabama, at Christmas, 1957, written in the Montgomery jail during the bus boycott. Reprinted in the A. J. Muste Essay Series, number 1 (A. J. Muste Memorial Institute, 339 Lafayette St., New York, NY 10012).

23. John Stoner, letter presented to the Kirkridge gathering of peace leaders, 1984.

24. Thomas Merton, *Conjectures of a Guilty Bystander* (Garden City, N.Y.: Doubleday, 1966), 56.

25. Bondurant, *Conquest of Violence,* 50.

26. Narayan Desai, letter to Françoise Pottier (January 27, 1986), courtesy of Richard Deats.

27. Milan Machovec, *A Marxist Looks at Jesus* (Philadelphia: Fortress Press, 1976), 108–9. In this regard, M. Scott Peck's otherwise remarkable book, *People of the Lie* (New York: Simon and Schuster, 1983), is flawed by his refusal to see the parents of his patients as themselves the victims of parents who were victims *ad infinitum.* As a consequence he demonizes people who also have a story that would evoke understanding and forgiveness if we only knew it. We are not contending against flesh and blood, but against the Powers: with the systems, structures, values, ideologies, and role images that make people the witting or

unwitting servants of the "father of lies." To put it bluntly, Jesus also died for the people of the lie, and all of us are such people.

28. Daniel Yergin, *Shattered Peace: The Origins of the Cold War and the National Security State* (Boston: Houghton Mifflin, 1977), 53.

29. Swomley, *Liberation Ethics,* 104.

30. Rob Robertson, "Response to the Kairos Document," quoted in Walter Wink, *Violence and Nonviolence in South Africa* (Philadelphia, Pa.: New Society, 1987), p. 69.

31. Allan Boesak, *Black and Reformed* (Johannesburg: Skotaville Publishers, 1984), 59.

32. Shelley Douglass, "Being Clear," *Ground Zero,* September/October, 1984.

33. "Before other men the man of free responsibility is justified by necessity; before himself he is acquitted by his conscience; but before God he hopes only for mercy" (Dietrich Bonhoeffer, *Ethics* [New York: Macmillan, 1963], 248).

34. John W. Swomley Jr., "Response to Gordon Zahn," *Fellowship* 43 (1977): 8.

35. Miguel D'Escoto, "An Unfinished Canvas," *Sojourners* (March 1983): 17.

36. Robertson, "Response to the Kairos Document."

37. "Nonviolence Wins the Philippines," Fellowship of Reconciliation leaflet (Box 271, Nyack, NY 10960).

38. Albert Camus, "Return to Tipasa," in *Lyrical and Critical Essays*, ed. Philip Thody. Trans. Ellen Conroy Kennedy (New York: Knopf, 1968), 165.

39. Richard Deats, "The Revolution That Didn't Just Happen," *Fellowship* 52 (July/August, 1986): 3–4; Peggy Rosenthal, "The Precarious Road," *Commonweal* (June 20, 1986): 364–67.

40. "Nonviolence Wins the Philippines."

41. Schell, "Reflections," 57.

Select Bibliography

Ackerman, Peter, and Christopher Kruegler. *Strategic Nonviolent Conflict: The Dynamics of People Power in the Twentieth Century.* Westport, Conn: Praeger, 1994.

Alinsky, Saul. *Rules for Radicals.* New York: Random House, 1971.

Berrigan, Daniel. *Steadfastness of the Saints: A Journal of Peace and War in Central and North America.* Maryknoll, N.Y.: Orbis, 1985.

Berquist, Jon L., ed. *Strike Terror No More: Theology, Ethics, and the New War.* St. Louis: Chalice, 2002.

Burggraeve, Roger, and Marc Vervenne, eds. *Swords into Plowshares: Theological Reflections on Peace.* Grand Rapids: Eerdmans, 1991.

Burns, J. Patout, ed. *War and Its Discontents: Pacifism and Quietism in the Abrahamic Traditions.* Washington, D.C.: Georgetown University Press, 1996.

Douglass, James W. *The Nonviolent Coming of God.* Maryknoll, N.Y.: Orbis, 1991.

———. *Resistance and Contemplation: The Way of Liberation.* Garden City, N.Y.: Doubleday, 1972.

Duffey, Michael K. *Peacemaking Christians: The Future of Just Wars, Pacifism, and Nonviolence.* Kansas City: Sheed & Ward, 1995.

Gandhi, Mahatma. *Non-violent Resistance (Satyagraha).* New York: Schocken, 1951.

Gish, Arthur G. *Hebron Journal: Stories of Nonviolent Peacemaking.* Scottdale, Pa.: Herald, 2001.

Givey, David W. *The Social Thought of Thomas Merton: The Way of Nonviolence and Peace for the Future.* Chicago: Franciscan Herald, 1983.

Guinan, Edward, ed. *Peace and Nonviolence: Basic Writings.* New York: Paulist, 1973.

Häring, Bernhard. *A Theology of Protest.* New York: Farrer, 1970.

Herr, Robert, and Judy Zimmerman Herr. *Transforming Violence: Linking Local and Global Peacemaking.* Scottdale: Herald, 1998.

Kässmann, Margot. *Overcoming Violence: The Challenge to the Churches in All Places.* Risk Book Series 82. Geneva: WCC Publications, 1998.

Kaufman, Gordon D. *Nonresistance and Responsibility, and Other Mennonite Essays.* Institute of

Mennonite Studies Series 5. Newton, Kans.: Faith and Life, 1979.

King, Martin Luther, Jr. "Loving Your Enemies." In *Strength to Love*. Philadelphia: Fortress Press, 1981.

Lachmund, Margarethe. *With Thine Adversary in the Way: A Quaker Witness for Reconciliation*. Translated by Florence L. Kite. Wallingford, Pa.: Pendle Hill, 1979.

Lakey, George. *Powerful Peacemaking: A Strategy for a Living Revolution*. Philadelphia: New Society, 1987.

Lynd, Staughton, and Alice Lynd, editors. *Nonviolence in America: A Documentary History*. Rev. ed. Maryknoll, N.Y.: Orbis, 1995.

McManus, Philip, and Gerald Schlabach. *Relentless Persistence: Nonviolent Action in Latin America*. Gabriola Island, B.C.: New Society, 1991.

Miller, William Robert. *Nonviolence*. New York: Schocken, 1972.

Moses, Greg. *Revolution of Conscience: Martin Luther King, Jr. and the Philosophy of Nonviolence*. Critical Perspectives. New York: Guilford, 1997.

Moyer, Bill. *Doing Democracy: The MAP Model for Organizing Social Movements*. Gabriola Island, B.C.: New Society, 2001.

Nagler, Michael N. *Is There No Other Way? The Search for a Nonviolent Future.* Berkeley: Berkeley Hills, 2001.

Pérez Esquivel, Adolfo. *Christ in a Poncho: Testimonials of the Nonviolent Struggles in Latin America.* Edited by Charles Antoine. Translated by Robert R. Barr. Maryknoll, N.Y.: Orbis, 1983.

Rosenberg, Marshall B. *Nonviolent Communication: A Language of Compassion.* Encinitas, Calif.: PuddleDancer, 2002.

Sharp, Gene. *The Politics of Nonviolent Action.* Extending Horizons Books. Boston: Sargent, 1973.

Soelle, Dorothee. *The Silent Cry: Mysticism and Resistance.* Translated by Barbara Rumscheidt and Martin Rumscheidt. Minneapolis: Fortress Press, 2001.

Stassen, Glen H. *Just Peacemaking: Ten Practices for Abolishing War.* Cleveland: Pilgrim, 1998.

———. *Just Peacemaking: Transforming Initiatives for Justice and Peace.* Louisville: Westminster John Knox, 1992.

Swartley, Willard M., ed. *Violence Renounced: René Girard, Biblical Studies, and Peacemaking.* Telford, Pa.: Pandora, 2000.

Trocmé, André. *Jesus and the Nonviolent Revolution.* Scottdale, Pa.: Herald, 1998.

Vanderhaar, Gerard D. *Active Nonviolence: A Way of Personal Peace.* Mystic, Conn.: Twenty-Third, 1990.

Wink, Walter. *Engaging the Powers: Discernment and Resistance in a World of Domination.* Minneapolis: Fortress Press, 1992.

———. *The Human Being: Jesus and the Enigma of the Son of the Man.* Minneapolis: Fortress Press, 2002.

———. *Naming the Powers: The Language of Power in the New Testament.* Minneapolis: Fortress Press, 1984.

———. *Peace Is the Way: Writings on Nonviolence from the Fellowship of Reconciliation.* Maryknoll, N.Y.: Orbis, 2000.

———. *Unmasking the Powers: The Invisible Forces that Determine Human Existence.* Philadelphia: Fortress Press, 1986.

———. *When the Powers Fall: Reconciliation in the Healing of Nations.* Minneapolis: Fortress Press, 1998.

The Fellowship
of Reconciliation

For further information contact:

Fellowship of Reconciliation
521 North Broadway
Nyack, NY 10960 USA
(845) 358-4601
http://www.forusa.org

International Fellowship of Reconciliation
Hof van Sonoy, 1811 LD
Alkmaar, The Netherlands
072.123.014
http://www.ifor.org